MW01602698

FOR BETTER

OR

FOR VERSE

JOAN PIERCE

To Mary Jo Love — Joan Pierce

This book is dedicated to all those family members for whom I have not yet written a verse.

Cover design by Katie Utter from an original oil painting by Joan Pierce

Copyright © 2014

ISBN-13: 978-1495942501
ISBN-10: 1495942503

Edition 1.0

Table of Contents

SEEKING

When I moved to the Catholic school in the 4th grade,
Sister rewarded us with holy cards. Most had a picture
of Jesus or Mary or a Saint and an appropriate short
prayer. Mine had no picture - just a purple border with
this anonymous verse inside:

O - a trouble's a ton
Or a trouble's an ounce
Or a trouble is what you make it
and it isn't the fact
that you're hurt that counts
But only how you take it.

All the grade school holy cards are long gone, but the
verse lives on - with unpretentious pleasure and
meaning.

May you find a few such lines here.

For Better

I know a poem needn't rhyme
But still, there needs to be
Timing of phrase to make words flow
Drawn by a current pulling past
Rocky outcrops round the bend
Neath toppled trees to waterfalls
That spray them down
Around the sound to meaning's end.

For Verse

Some people think in verse.
Terse metered rhythms
Nurse a thought and make it shine.
A line of words
Entwine new meanings like
Thin vines that weave and climb
Sublime in sweet meanderings
Of rhyme.

Place

A small space with light is what I seek
A place for me to pray, to write, to strain
To once more hear the unfamiliar creak
Of inspiration walking in my brain.
There I shall meet myself again but more,
For God's own Love will open wide the door.
So I shall enter peace I can't create
Where time and space no longer operate.
There all alone, yet linked to everyone
I'll know that God is here, my work begun.

Continuity

Life loops a thread
That has led me to the here and the now
In a bow tied by continuity.

It is a silken skein
That slides along as I creep on
And it is strong because a mother
Fed me with care on mulberry leaves.

It is a tow rope
Splashing through warm waves of youth
And I hang on until knees collapse,
The boat is gone and I fall in.

It is a tightrope strung
From business to success and I
Must keep my balance lest I die.

It is a tape that
Winds down the other spool.
Speed limit should be 55
But it is hard to tell.

The coil that
Courses round and round
To the still deep eternal whence I came
Was not the same, then.

It is a loop of mystery
At the core where time slows spinning
While I weave the loose ends in
To the beginning.

5

The Generation Circle

Grandma came to America
On an immigrant ship
Carrying her belongings in a quilt.

Mother married a farmer
And milked and planted
To raise me so that

I could come to town
To get an education
And pass on the finer things to

My daughter who isn't sure
That college is relevant and
Has gone backpacking in Europe.

Color Today

**My week was multicolored
Minnesota Frieze in Honolulu hues**

Color Sunday white
All possibility combined yet undefined
The white, bright Light of the Spirit.

Color Monday orange
The fire of all resolutions begun
A new-kindled flame that flares as it bursts.

Color Tuesday yellow
Warm summer sunshine
The easy after glow of yesterday.

Color Wednesday green
No sick sterile hallway
The lush of tropical forest.

Color Thursday blue
The patch of warm sky, not moody,
The ocean vast, welcoming deep.

Color Friday red
Highlight of the five day work week
Celebrated from McDonald's to the moon.

Saturday is brown
Murky combinations of garden weeds and other chores
Bronzed bodies lolling on the beach.

Color my life
Stark neon psychedelic
Or gentle rainbow hues
Only black,
Lightless black never choose.

7

Please

Don't cry me a river
Bleed sorrow for lust
Just tell me a rainbow
And lie if you must.

Dreams

I had a dream that I could be
a person of reality.
I had a dream that I could see
truth shining from inside of me.
I had a dream that I could stand alone,
yet clothed in love that shone
on others like a warm, soft veil
hiding all that's weak and frail from curious eyes.
I dreamed that people could redeem
the dreams that never came to be,
and minds that float the salted sea
of superficiality.

GRAMMAR

Verbs

I AM, God says.
We creatures just participate
In Being -- the great All in All.

I have, we say.
Words that quickly separate,
Precipitate old Adam's Fall.

Nouns

On all the earth from whence we came
Each one of us has his own name
To show that we are not the same.
So while we live, we play the game
And aim to win, to seek for fame
To be the one with the biggest name.

12

Comma

A comma is the writer's attempt to put a pause between words.
I can savor life with a pause.

A comma requires no strong mind like: That's it period, does;
No inquiring into the other like question or quotation marks
No pretensions like a colon or semi-colon to impress a novice
more than the bureaucratic word.

A comma announces another idea's forthcoming,
It lives with lists, qualifiers, the dependent clause.

It's ordinary, therein lies its potential.
Great novels are written with ordinary words.
A Mai Tai may seem exotic but a bit of rum --
unlimited possibilities.

Grammarians have thought up rules for using commas.
But even they are forced to admit
Great writers use commas at will
To bring out the sense of a passage.

I like to read with the pause that comes from
A little comma sense.

Fact or Fiction

Sometimes I tell myself the heartfelt story
Of who I think I am and used to be
Could some biographer paint a true picture
If I still wonder who is really me?
How should I change my story's primal focus
To fit these eyes so they can clearly see
This introvert, extrovert persona
The I in my autobiography.

Generation Gap

My daughter buys just wash 'n wear.
She cannot comprehend
That Tuesday used to be the day
I ironed to the end.

I tried to make her understand
That chore was Purgatory.
It didn't help. She'd never heard
The Purgatory story.

Image

When I was a girl, I was sloppy.
It took years of hard work to convert
To a coiffured, deodorized lady
And two months of running to revert.
Now I sweat from my hair to my toenails
And wipe my nose on the end of my shirt.

Gender

Does the sun shine on the plant
With a definite feminine slant
So it grows a little bit askew?
Is there a masculine path that's true?
Perhaps no beam is meant to be
Complete as one or even two
But all of us together see
The Christ enfleshed eternally.

SEASONS

Arizona Green

Arizona Green

Carpets brown desert mountains

In pale springtime hues.

Sentinel Saguaros stand

Guarding sundrenched empty land.

Here

I picture life along some country road
Fragrant with the spring.
I dream of God in open space and lakes
Of blue remembering.

I wade in memory of time when days were new
And months were long
And guardian angels floated round to block temptation
Till I grew strong.

Now there are two trees in our yard
Mock orange grows next door.
God finds me still the moment that
I let my spirit soar.

The First of June

May came
Without a spring
Just ice and slush
And more raining
Till I got used to it
And quit complaining.

But it is June
A blaze of yellow flowers
Postcard blue sky
I don't know how
to encompass
The perfectness of now.

Lord, plant in me
Some holy leaven
That can expand my soul
And make me capable
Of heaven.

June

It is June.
I must leave my bed to look northeast
Where rose reflections rise
Behind the trees.

I would be at the lake
And see it over water reflecting all the richness
To make it twice as orange and pink and gold
Beside the blue.

Or gazed through the back window of the car
Heading toward Wyoming
Across the brown rolling west land
Past the sand and water crossings of the Platte.

I am not a morning person in my life
But for vacation I arise
To celebrate my soul for seeing
It is June.

"Therefore, on every morrow, are we wreathing
A flowery band to bind us to the earth"
-John Keats - *A Thing of Beauty*

Bands

I would stay here forever in June
Here in my house by my pine
Walking to Lake Phalen that daily changes
And the full moon setting in the pre-dawn pallor of the
sky.

I would stay here forever
In the campgrounds by the rivers
Where the current carries my yellow canoe
Through time.

I would sit beside the shores
Of lakes I've know at Isle O'Pine,
Darling, Trout, Itasca -
Mine, all mine in memory,
In wonder, in every year the differentness
Of June.

Yes, I would stay here forever
But forever isn't mine.
Life is a fine stream of consciousness
That flows and trickles and freezes over
Complete, I suppose in some unknown plan
I seldom see

Though I believe that I too draw it,
Tone it, where it goes is me,
(for that I came).

June is so short here
A few perfect mornings
And warm evenings that extend
Outside my window as lights come on
For reading words that bind the band.

Midnight Swim

Long set sun still steeps its warmth
In water near the shore.
A path of moonbeam aims my way,
I step onto the sandy floor
And dive into a path of light.
Smooth stroke, sometimes I float
Across the bay and back.
Then I must once more face the air,
Crouch and tuck wet shoulders under
Till I rise and square them
As a Spartan bold
Who never flinches in the cold.

Petunias

They stood tall in proud purple profusion
Before humbling rain strained purple
From these chastened trembling flowers
Gone faded and limp into the starless night.

Now morning sunlight dries the drops.
Pink faces arch to greet the light.
Though smaller, paler, they return,
Signs of the deeper shade within.

Morning

October enters through east-facing windows
And turns my glass top table to mirror lake.
Blue sky beneath last red oak leaves
Frames skinny birch still strained to summer sun
Turned upside down across the glass to me.

At the Lake

Lone loon remains in late October
Dives in rippling blue
Too young and left behind
To journey on his own.
How will he know
Which way to go
Or when he's fully grown.

Autumn

Whipping, whining, willful, wheeling, whirling,
whishing, wintry wind
Sweeps sun-kissed summer swift away.
Just yesterday we walked in calm bright warmth
And played at lithesome lovely life.
Now cloud upon cloud, scarce rays slip through
Reducing the sky from blissful blue to dark'ning gray.
Gold, crimson and green, the maples swing
Leaves curl, still cling for autumn is young.
So abrupt the shift that brings in cold
Overwhelms a spirit suddenly old.

The Power Failure

I lost Thursday in my kitchen
Huddled in a rocker
By the open oven door
Wrapped in quiet with no clicking
Of appliances to signal
That my work was being done.

There Willa Cather led me
Through the red grass of Nebraska
To my Grandma in the wheat fields
And a single room log cabin
Locked in days when life was stillness
Before Thomas Edison.

Winter Wish

I want to stay warm within
when the snow falls;
return to the day of childhood
when weather kept me home from school.
And find some use for
my preserved peaches and apples and pears.
I want to watch white nature
and succumb to peace.

I could stand winter
if I could just stand it.
But everyone around me shouts out NO.
Plow the streets
Drive to work
Keep your appointment
Shop and carry home.

I want to sit inside in winter
Bake cookies, read stories, cook soup
Till the sun melts ice and I can step
into hints of spring out on my stoop.

Yesterday's Sun

Then you came at five o'clock
(after I'd labored in gloom all day)
filling my room with yellow, gold, red.
"Need a heap of clouds for great sunsets,"
the Yellowstone Park Ranger said.
You've done this before, burst forth to surprise.
Too late for picnics, I thought
and hurried to plan the tomorrow, instead
of welcoming you with warm gracious heart.
I thought you augured a clear dawn
but I was wrong. You make no promises.

SOJOURNS

Egypt

Isis had a crisis
When Tutankhamen came.
Long lines of slender ladies
Attested to his fame.

The Sphinx lay in the desert
Unable to arise.
The camel driver drove his beasts
And tourists, I surmise.

No epic tales the Pharaohs told
But giants in the sand
Still speak antiquity to us
Who yearn to view their land.

Paris

What can one do with a memory?
Can I see all those hours again?
The steps that come up to the Motte Piquet
From the Metro that linked to the plane.

See the room opened up in front of the stair
See the window, the bed and the closet door
A flower, two chocolates welcome us in
To our tiny space on the second floor.

What we dream of Paris are the bridges
That cross and recross the Seine
The bateau mouche on the river
The quais for walking there once again.

The Dutchman said: If there's a choice
Paris is the place to be.
How many churches in Paris,
How many cafes do we see?

Each visit to Paris is different
Yet something still stays the same.
We come a bit older and wiser
And feel true love's flickering flame.

Prague

Three travelers on a journey
With no mission but to stare
At historic pink stone buildings
Ears open to the air
Of foreign spoken syllables
Mid tourists everywhere.

We heard the opera legend
Of Lebuse and Premysl
Climbed up to the beer garden
For great Pilsner Urquil.
Saw numerous goulash places
Found one that fit the bill.

We crossed Vltava River
On Charles' famous bridge
While studying the statues
Then climbing to the ridge
Where castle and cathedral
Filled us with awe and glee
We walked and talked the days were full
Of joy to be we three.

ND Football Game

Sunny Indiana mid-October
It's a football Saturday at Notre Dame.
To celebrate alum extended family
Seems more important even than the game.
I look around at all the happy people
This day they're exactly where they want to be.
Whence comes that spirit that we all are into?
Crowds make way, long lines wait patiently.

Parking lots are filled with folks tailgating
Young boys toss footballs down wide blacktop aisles,
Body-guarded coach and suit clad players
Parade across bright campus, all the while
The band assembles, rows on rows all ready
Shiny gold brass decorates their navy blue
The fight song erupts, we follow our Pied Pipers
Game starts, now cheering is the work we came to do.

In the City

If a world can someday cataclypse
Into a thick black hole,
Can I pour out by bits of self
(Dream and habit, face and role)
Into an asphalt pot to melt
And hope to come out whole?

Hugh Norris Trail

We went walking in the hills
And hiked the rock strewn way.
Saguaro stood unbending there
Mid shrubs of green and gray.

We climbed on sand, then stony steps
Switchbacking in the shade,
Then round to sun soaked mountainside,
Tucson's winter masquerade.

A raven circled like a hawk
Then lit on sandstone cliff.
His mate was settled just above
They posed jet black and stiff.

The shadows lengthen down the wash
While white stones turn to shade.
And up the cactus spotted hill
Six gambol quails parade.

Out here the present moment lives
In silence, stretched beyond
All sound of cars or daily stress.
Sunset seals Nature's bond.

Tucson Silence

I lift my eyes to the mountains
Blue sky, palo verde tree,
Sun on pink brick glows into evening
This is a quiet place.

And I am quiet too seeking silence
I look out but want to see within
Wisdom, Word, You Cosmic Christ
Breath of life, heart of all right here.

MYSTERIES

A Word to the Music

I wonder why I cannot hear
The music of the cosmic sphere.

I ask you, God, is there a way?
You walked as man on earth, they say.
Then why did you not answer
The questions of today--
Or your own day? When you were here
You spoke in parable.
Why would you not declare the words
That we so want to hear?

He who has ears to hear, let him hear:

I am not tuned, fine-tuned to
High cross of love transmitter.
I prefer to buy a system,
One that's current, tasteful, true
And mold a gold antenna line
From my storeroom of fine things
So I can hold it high above the hill.
Then I could fly and fly until
I'd hear my dream come true.

He who has ears to hear, let him hear:

God, are you there? Can you teach me
All I need to know?
I concentrate so hard to hear
That silence makes a break through fear.
From deep the faintest whisper breathes,
"Let go your rod. Dare to be free.
Unclench your fist. Let go, let go."

42

I whisper, "No." That can't be right.
I'm not a fool. Adjust the sound.
Turn up control.

I wonder why I cannot hear
The music of the cosmic sphere.

Universe

O for that three tiered universe
Where Dante trekked dark paths in verse.
Then heaven was close above the earth.
Angels flew in for death and birth.
Hell too was near, down underneath
With screams and fires and gnashing teeth.
Though life was short and work was hard
Churches kept sinful man on guard.

Now everything is different
Nothing is clear--Ought we repent?
Our vistas are of vastness and
No master plan to understand.
Though physically we live in ease
Amazement only serves to tease
The minds of all who seek to know
Where are we now, where will earth go?

Resurrection

T'was the middle of summer on East Bayside Drive
Hardly a man or a woman alive
Wasn't shut in his house out of fear.

A purple green light came out of the sky.
The waves of the bay were rising up high.
The wind was a blast in the ear.

In the center of town, the mayor gave a shout,
"Let's round up some trucks to get people out
If the disaster that threatens strikes here."

They phoned and they hurried and they assembled a
crew.
Then the mayor said, "Now if we knew what to do
We could get our operation in gear."

Meanwhile, above the water a missile descended.
From under the sea rose a huge bulk upended,
A remnant of long yesteryear.

The mysterious galleon lurched up into sight
And the missile hovered over and drew it upright
Like the future attracting a seer.

As the galleon and missile joined together in one
Huge metal monster that weighed more than a ton
From the air came a tone long and clear.

It signaled the townsfolk to turn out to sea
And each man, unbelieving, unable to flee
Stood transfixed by his eye and his ear.

45

And the sight and the sound that before was so scary
Now seemed so sublime, so mellow, so airy
That there was not a trace left of fear.

And the colors all merged like some giant rainbow
And the missile now rose to the clouds all aglow
And pulled the ship to some heavenly sphere.

Then the wind stopped a blowing from out of the deep
But the people walked softly as though still asleep
With a dream the whole town dreamed one year.

September 11th

September 11--Ten years to the day.
We watch towers fall--Repeat the play.
Holding fast to our belief
There's nobility in grief
While blind to true heart knowing
What pain our bombs are sowing.

Simple Dreams

Scientists tell us that maybe
There's something that's faster than light.
Probably soon they'll tell us
There's something that's brighter than bright.
They're not locked into their senses
The way that most of us are.
They dream up new focus for seeing
A universe too terribly far
From what we can dream or discover
With our less probing sort of a mind
That searches just peace for our planet
And hopes above all to be kind.

Ash Wednesday

Ash Wednesday, yesterday of fast and penitence,
Of resolutions formed and stomach empty.
For all my reckonings, what does God care
If what I do is hard? Is it for Him?
How does He gain by my discomfiture?
No, only I who learn that I can live without
Such ease as I've grown used to having.
That's the key. The wanting, needing, grasping
Must be dissolved in me. Then can I choose
Unenslaved by habit having, destined to be free.

49

Channel

"Lord, make me a channel of your peace"

From stone walled narrow canyon
To alluvial fertile plain
The River of Life flows to the sea
And rains back down again.
The glorious, unknown, unseen God
Is so close like a mother
Whose unborn child is part of her
And yet is wholly other.
The genes of true divinity
Carried through her birth
Are more than outside influence,
The stamp of human worth.
From first beginning she will be
A conduit for precious gifts,
And as she grows and searches life,
The pathway necessarily shifts,
Saints may endure the River's flooding,
But we just seek to know and grow
In love and strength our God provides
If we are open to the flow.

Negotiations

Wind whips the wires
That hang from house to pole
Violence vibrates voices
That shift from role to role.
Nature isn't peaceful
Or even kind.
If all is a reflection
Of the immortal mind
Can we really make a difference
By the breath that births our soul?
Will people's plans make peace when
Destruction seems earth's goal?

Superbowl 2013

We took hell out of our churches
And hoped it would just disappear.
We were wrong. It is here
Displayed in fire and brimstone pyrotechnics,
Expensive glamorous violence and sex
On a giant screen in your family room,
The great American cultural event of the year.

Whence will the barbarians come
To topple Rome's new Coliseums,
Super domes,
And rescue our indoctrinated children
From values of pleasure and guns?
Will a new Moses lead a little band
From the fleshpots to the Promised Land?
Or a new Martin Luther King
Profess a dream that will unite
Random kindness into a stream
To baptize a community clean
From manufactured horror, deadly fear?

And You Shall be My Witness

"And you shall be my witness"

How can I be your witness, Lord
If you keep eluding me?
How could I preach of heaven's bliss
Out of hope's obscurity?

I stand in earth stained rags of faith
Rigid with doubt, and fear
That I won't hear your call to life.
Oh Lord, unclench my ear.

LOVE

Promise

Self is the mausoleum
Where eyes gaze always in
But satin cannot silence
The exiled spirit's plan.

The scent of freedom mingles
With aloes and myrrh
Strength seeps through stony crevices
From love outside the door.

Regret

Some days it seems so strange
That Mother and Dad aren't here.
How have I really changed
In these intervening years?
Is it all about my childhood
Or the last time we were near
Each other when we would
Share happy thoughts 'cause Mother clearly
Saw life through a bright rosy lens:
Anticipation, seldom fear.
So often I just merely took
Them for granted, didn't hear
The untold need behind soft gaze
That said, "We love you, dear."

Care

Through pain a moment flickers
I turn outself to see
One spark of unsought giving
Unmasks eternity.

Contentment

I am content with sitting here
Beside the windowed gray spring day
To know that I have somewhere I must go
But not too soon
Not this quiet afternoon.

I am content with books around me
Drawing, Kenya, Lewis, Mann
To know that I can dabble, choose, and change.
Not that I must finish for a reason
Beyond the joy of reading season.

I am content with cooking smells
Bread and cake and roasting chicken
To know I've cleaned up all the mess
I am content this day alone.
Knowing my love will come back home.

I Love You

I love you as I hold your hand across the rocks or down a hill
I love you as you hold my hand just to be near or nearer still
I love you as I see, through years, your khaki pants, blue sweater
I love you as I see you now and feel love's even better.
I love you when you smile or laugh or look into my eyes
And share the moment full of joy that comfortably ties
Our hearts together, interweaving days
Of light and darkness, clear with haze.
They form our pattern, that one "we"
That's made our life and family.
I love you as you light the candles, pour the wine,
Clean up my messy cooking,
I love you as your kindness shows
When I'm not even looking.
I love you with my body, mind and spirit –
All that's me.
I love all that is so obvious
And all I seldom see.
I love you from the depth where God leads both of us together
I love you in my winter days and here in sun filled weather
I love you as we seek a dream too precious to be real
I love you in the dust and grime and blood and itch we feel.
I love you in the grandest way that great occasions muster
I love you in the daily sameness without pomp or bluster
I love you in the quiet of the evening sunset glow
I love you truly more than I can really know.
I love you without words, in silent meditation
I love you in our family, each coming generation
I love you in a way that's impossible to bend
This litany of thoughts into a poem that ever ends.

Winter 1999, Tucson

60

To John Donne: Shadows

We walked the steps past shadows
Those days we read your poems.
Knew love in that full constant light
That grew and brightened with the years.

Now I am here and walk alone
In some uncharted part of day
Perhaps twilight, but not yet night
Death mustn't mean true love's decay.

GROWING

64th Birthday

This isn't a milestone, I know that
It's just one more rock on the pile
But I find that I face a new question:
Can I still go with the flow for a while?
Or has the time come now to settle?
Or will I simply be settling for less?
What is 'more' in this antique equation-
Too-tight-jeans or an outmoded dress?

Sure Thing

Who knew that truth involved a lifelong search
When we weren't the ones who asked the questions?
We learned the right words and thought that our
church
Would hide our ignorance from detection.

So now we're old and life has slowed with time
To recall the question that then seemed clear;
Where is God? We answered: He's everywhere.
I still struggle to find everywhere here.

Far Sighted

I got glasses so I could see
Things that were right in front of me.

My eyes have always gazed afar
At the new horizon and morning star.
My heart had dreams that led me to
Tahiti, Rome and Timbuktu.

But often I've neglected life,
The here and now, the work and strife,
And said, "Next year and over there
I'll thrive content without a care."

But now I'm older and I find
(Though I can't leave all dreams behind)
That I must live this day or lose it,
That love only grows when I dare choose it.

I got glasses so I could see
Things were all right in front of me.

Wisdom

Back in my young life when I knew that I knew
Aristotle and Thomas led me toward God.
They had answers to questions: the good and the true.
Life meant a disciplined race to the place
Of Infinite Majesty known face to face.

Now I am old and watch more, answer less.
St. Francis, the dreamer, has helped with the stress
Of being so right and so driven by rules.
Now trusting the wonderful gifts I've been given
My goal is to join with God's holy fools.

Success

The journey wasn't over
When I reached the mountaintop.
The mist concealed deep valleys
And a road that didn't stop.

Now though I walk more slowly
I dare leave the well marked trail
To roam the desert star night
Or face a test and fail.

Too Late

Dreams contain an element
Of talent unfulfilled.
Guilt stalks grow tall in fertile fields
That never will be tilled.

The Verdict

The medic calls the process diagnosis
While the patient, me, sits in the guilty chair.
Self-accused the symptoms are spilled out
Like jigsaw pieces on a bare
Glass table top.

This healthy fit body still feels like me
While muscles atrophy, speech slurs.
Where did my arm muscles go?
How can words come out so slowly?
What we called possibility
Is fact. I know before the verdict's given.

The sentence sounds like two to ten.
With little help for good behavior.
Support is here, the doctors says,
To move distressed and mixed-up pieces
Around on your glass table top.

Horizons

Once you're old you have to know
That you'll get something someday
To lay you low and lead you on
Beyond to life's soon ending way.
Though faith and hope both promise
A fuller, brighter, happier day,
This earth does not seem dark enough
To yearn to sail the spirit's way.

Kingdom

The kingdom of heaven is now, Jesus said
So I'm happy with love life each day
Though I know that there's an end in sight
Inevitable passing away,
I figured that was the future
And suddenly the future's too near.
How can I live so intensely
That Love will banish all fear?

Hearing Aids

I grew up with a fear of sticking things in my ear
Now mornings I swim with ear plugs plugged in
And evenings I listen to voices made clear
By aides I paid dearly to stick in my ear.

The Sneeze

Once I could feel it coming on
Like a locomotive slowed on two tracks
Steam exuding in one final spurt.

Now with this day's disease,
I explode to my disbelief
No warning call
The burst engulfing all
Overwhelming sense like love or grief.

Growing Old

For all the new beginnings
What have I to show?
For all the fires that I have lit
I'll settle for the glow
That Love eternal kindled
That day I let him in
When I finally saw my neighbor's fear
And forgot about his sin.

Visitors

Fine fall afternoon faded
As visitors came to see me today
Bearing cabbage roses and lavender stalks
White petals wrapped in vegetable leaves
Like three widows' homely memories.

We plucked out petals
From mutual pasts when there were six
Biking, hiking, dining and those last days
When we lost them one by one
Each to his own oblivion.

Now winter's coming
And we know that we won't brave the season
Alone to drive mid sleet and snow.
Dare we go south to wait for spring--
The question hangs, none answering.

Beyond the Round

I fit eternity into a line
That circled through forgotten past
Ahead to link the future
In a dot called I and Now.
But lines are narrow.

I fit eternity into a globe
To round it out
And perched upon my spot like North America
Convinced of its importance to the world.
But globes are hollow.

I fit eternity into a ball
To give it depth
And pushed myself like a diameter
Through thick dark airless mass
But balls do bounce.

Only death will serve the final thrust
To shoot me clear beyond this round
That blocks my way.
I cannot scale eternity
To fit the finite me.

OCCASIONS

Wishes

I wish I were a poet
With a hundred birthday rhymes.
I wish I were a player
Of an organ with bell chimes.
I wish I were a singer
With a song of tender wishes.
I wish I were a French chef
Making gastronomic dishes.
But since it isn't probable
That all our dreams come true,
I'll just say HAPPY BIRTHDAY
And wish good dreams for you.

Mother's Day

There isn't any reason why
I shouldn't look so proud.
Those folks I met just said to me
In voices clear and loud,
"Why, you're just like your mother,
I'd know you anywhere."
(I feared at first that they could see
the gray strands in my hair.)

But then they said, "You sound like her
and make us feel at ease.
You smile and laugh and frown like her
and do just as you please."
Then I knew that they could see
The things that make my mother
And if I am like anyone
I'd not choose any other.

Ollie

We'd like to say something different
That's novel, exciting and bold
To celebrate your happy birthday
And make it a fete to behold.
But what that would be we can't fathom
The secrets we held are all told.
So we'll stick with our song
"Happy Birthday"
While all the young voices unfold
The words like a gem or a grandpa
Grow more precious as they get old.

You say that you don't want a present
So what is a daughter to do
With a father who's always so loving
And kind and considerate too?

We wanted to give you a golf swing
That Nicklaus would pause to admire
Or a magnificent piano concerto
That Bernstein would say was afire.

But since you don't want a present
We'll just have to share what we own
Hearts full of love and affection
From the family and Leo and Joan.

82

Tony - 1990

We're glad you have a birthday
The same time every year
Or else how would each great new age
Periodically appear?

We're glad that you've invited us
To celebrate with you
Or else, where would our wishes go?
What would our present do?

For 13 years you've been around
And we can truly say
We love you and we hope for you
A year of perfect days.

Lindsey

We came to the townhouse in Tucson
To meet this new baby girl,
Your parents took turns all night trying
To soothe our sweet babe who kept crying.

When Lauren was born, we stayed longer
Discovered your favorite thing
And Grandpa and I took turns pushing
You in your own little swing.

We hiked in Sabino Canyon
Where you were three, maybe four
After the dryer had finished
Drying the one dress you wore.

I marveled at your wide set eyes,
Foresaw the beauty that you'd be,
Met your friends, you welcomed us
Into your life so graciously.

I remember New Year's Eve at our house,
Special yogurt each Friday night.
We watched you swim and violin
With pride and joy, our shining light.

And now you've finished college
Embarking on a new career.
Thank you Linds, for being you.
I'm just thrilled that we are here.

Connie

I was glad you were a girl
Petite--just the right size
For darling designer dresses,
Bernie's daughter's bright surprise,
A wardrobe for a princess
Shining in daddy's eyes.

Do you remember grade school?
For me it's now a haze.
I think I made you take your lunch
At least, on winter days.
Did you get good at running then?
What was your favorite phrase?

You went to all the hockey games,
Cheer-led for us at home,
Played basketball and tennis,
Found out the need to roam
To happy new warm vistas
Replete with surf and foam.

I think you resemble Grandma
Love a guy who keeps making you proud,
Excel at cards and golf and friendliness,
Plan parties for a fun family crowd,
Make vacations the best yearly highlight,
Voice opinion, but never too loud.

Should I have done some things different?
Pushed higher education for you?
Whatever mistakes that I made then
You came through so wonderfully true
A daughter I love sharing life with
Your presence, what you say, all you do.

Mary Ellen

Named for two great grandmothers
Both lived for ninety years
From days of horse and buggies
To automatic gears.

Grandma Mary widowed early
Had to make her way
She had faith in her ideas
And always had her say.

Grandma Ellen was a seeker
Finally settled on
The Adventists who said this world
Will surely soon be gone.

She helped raise the four grandchildren
Who admired her no end
She welcomed all the relatives
And was a true Godsend.

And now that you've reached middle life
May you still take a clue
From these who went before you
And loved the little girl they knew.

32nd Year

Our wishes aren't fishes
That just float away
Our pictures come true
They portray what we say.

So we're painting a talented,
Musical hue
For your greatest year ever
When you're thirty-two.

Happy Birthday!

40th Birthday

Forty--that's the number
When they say that life begins
But those of us who've passed it know
How fast each new year spins.

Think of it as a midway mark
That came on pretty slow
You may not yet be ready
But now the time will go
So fast you may not notice
(If you're not perceptive-plus)
That hourglass ran overtime
And you've caught up to us.

Mike - 1985

How wonderful to be your age
The prime of life, they say--
You're young enough to look just great
And wise enough to pray;
Old enough to know your mind,
Ready to think or speak;
Strong enough to hold your son;
Athletic--at your peak.
So have your happiest birthday
For that's how it will be.
The prime of life is thirty-two
Until you're thirty-three.

To John Utter:

We knew you were the kind of guy
Who'd have to really really try
To figure out why we would buy
The stupid cards we've seen.

To spend two bucks ain't a big deal
But when the jokes are so surreal
And sentiments are fake, we feel
What can they even mean?

So we've composed this little verse
To say, for better or for worse
We hope late greetings to reimburse
At Nisswa Dairy Queen

(Wouldn't you rather have a blizzard?)

90

Denise – 2010

I'd like to make Beef Stroganoff
And drink white wine with you
But now we aren't in Tucson
And we bear a woe or two
So when we ask the question
Lord, what am I to do?
Know we're here for one another
Like a tried, faithful crew
To sail thru any weather
Across days bright or blue
So lift a glass to happy thoughts
I send all mine to you.

Piecing – February 2, 1996

I always thought piecing
Meant making a quilt
By pioneer ladies
Who our nation built.
But last night our piecing
Found a far better way
With hot spinach veg dip
And mango sorbet.
We fashioned a gentle new
Friendship with cheer.
Your wisdom foresaw it
We thank you, Jean dear.

Jean Drury invited Leo and me to meet her friends,
the Bremers. Instead of formal dinner, Jean called
our hors d'oeuvres "piecing".

Jean Drury, March 18, 1999

Could you ever really have imagined
These days when we've both come "of age ?"
Had we foreseen our distant futures
Would we be turning a different page?

Thank God we just live in our present
Each stage an adventure to share
And if jeans won't cover the midriff
Sagacity vows not to care.

Just so we still keep on growing
In mind and in spirit, I mean
And I stay your oldest friend Joannie
And you - my inestimable Jean.

To Katie-

How could we leave you an orphan
Without this bright emblem to wear?
When we're filled with such love for each other
Memories of our trip everywhere.
We know just who's who by the colors
The coppery maiden is you.
The generation that binds us together
Is Kate donned in warm golden hue
And I am the silvery other
Thrilled to fill the grandmother role
As we've traveled to share and discover
Sweet Prague and dear Budapest's soul.

In 2011, Katie Avila, Katie Utter and I celebrated their
birthdays and my Mother's Day in Prague. Katie A.
gave Katie and me a pin depicting three ladies, so
after coming home, we bought one for her.

Harry Camp

How can we explain that you
Would live to one hundred and three?
I think it's due to your finding
Myrna on that ship out at sea.

And maybe you need a lifetime
To share love at every stage
So you've made the most of your second youth
Now you're just entering middle age.

Some day—not yet—you'll have to reach
Old age, like the rest of us.
For now have a happy birthday
Dear Harry, you are tremendous.

2013

Domenic Leo on His Baptism Day

St. Dominic came from Spain and founded
The Black Friars with a mission to preach.
He lived in poverty, fought corruption
Sent faithful followers worldwide to teach.

History knew saintly popes named Leo
The first saved Rome from Attila the Hun
Most were scholars, art lovers and thinkers
Leo the thirteenth, the most famous one.

You're descended from two strong great grandpas
Bohemia and Italy flavored each name.
They lived up to their sainted namesakes
A hundred years before ever you came.

Think of all of those Doms who are praying
With holy Leos in their heavenly club.
They'll see you through days that are peaceful
And guide you through all life's hubbub.

Now here are your very own grandpas
Bestowing artistic, scholarly traits.
You have models enough for a squadron
With godparents truly first rate.

With all of these wonderful blessings
There's nothing can ever outdo
The love that four grandmas are sending
Dear Domenic Leo to you.

96

Tradition

We're a most unmusical family
Except for an in-law or two
But Grandma's favorite holiday pastime
Is singing – so what do you think we do?

We sing carols, of course, for Christmas
Deck the Halls, Silent Night, Drummer Boy.
Edelweiss, Bless This House for Thanksgiving
And so we all share in the joy

Of standing round circled together
Our various voices to raise
To you, Lord, love's great provider,
Old songs of our joy and our praise.

97

9437808R00061

Made in the USA
San Bernardino, CA
15 March 2014